Slow Cooker Soups and Stews

Easy, Simple and Delicious Beef, Chicken, Vegetable and Much More!

Contents

Introduction:

Crock pots and soup recipes are made for each other. The slow cooking process extracts maximum flavor from chicken, beef, vegetables, or any other ingredients added into it. Beyond soup, a slow cooker is great for stew. Low-watt heat surrounds the food to bring it gently to the peak of perfection. In addition to enjoying better flavor, healthier meals, and saving money on meats and electricity, you will have more leisure time. No turning, no stirring, no adjusting heat, no timing to the minute. Just start the slow cooker and head out for the day! Leave your slow cooker alone all day, or all night; it's perfectly safe with its low wattage. The flavors blend nicely to give it a wholesome earthy flavor that is unbelievably.

Disclaimer

Disclaimer and Terms of Use: Effort has been made to ensure that the information in this book is accurate and complete, however, the author and the publisher do not warrant the accuracy of the information, text and graphics contained within the book due to the rapidly changing nature of science, research, known and unknown facts and internet. The Author and the publisher do not hold any responsibility for errors, omissions or contrary interpretation of the subject matter herein. This book is presented solely for motivational and informational purposes only.

About the Book

What's your favorite slow cooker soup? Chicken stew, potato soup, beef stew, vegetable soup, or another classic -- here you'll find all the best soups and stews that come warm and bubbly from your slow cooker. This book is for those people who want to use the slow cooking process to extract maximum flavor from chicken, beef, vegetables, and pork. These dishes have been prepared with careful attention to the ingredients and how the flavors combine in the crock pot. Cozy up with slow cooker soups that will warm you right up from head-to-toe.

Enjoy this collection of recipes specifically created for people who want to try some flavorful dishes slow-cooked to release all the flavors from each ingredient.

Each recipe is carefully crafted for preparation in the crock pot.

Easy to make and delicious tasting soups and stews.

Enjoy slow cooked soups and stews which are good for your health.

BEEF

Slow-Cooker Classic Beef Stew

Serves 8-10

1 c. dry red wine

6-ounce tomato paste

2 c. onions

1/3 c. olive oil

1 c. all-purpose flour

4 lbs. bottom round

1 c. frozen peas

1 tsp. dried thyme leaves

1/2 lb. baby carrots

1 bay leaf

2 c. beef broth

4 c. Potatoes

1 tbsp. kosher salt

Start by heating up oil in the frying pan on medium to high heat. Then cover the beef in flour. Add the beef until it is thoroughly browned. Once browned, add it to the slow cooker. In a clean skillet, sauté the onions until softened and add them to the crockpot with the tomato paste. Then add in the wine and remaining ingredients except for the peas. Cook for 7 hours on the low setting. Lastly 10 minutes before serving, add the peas. Then enjoy!

French Country Beef Stew

Serves 6

1⁄2 c. parsley

2 tsp. extra-virgin olive oil

2 c. dry red wine

11⁄2 c. carrots

1 tsp. fresh thyme leaves

1⁄2 c. celery

1 1⁄2 c. chopped onion

4 slices turkey bacon

3 c. beef broth

31⁄2-33⁄4 lb. sliced beef shank

2 orange zest 2 1⁄2-inch

2 bay leaves

Pepper To taste

Start by heating the oil for 5 minutes. Then add the vegetables and cook for 8 minutes. Boil broth, wine, thyme, bay leaves and orange zest. Combine the beef and hot vegetable mixture and cook for 6 to 7 hours. Break the meat into 2 to 3 inch chunks with a spoon. Remove the bay leaves and orange zest from the sauce. Boil the sauce. Boil, skimming for about 20 minutes and season with pepper. Add the beef and heat through. Add watercress to serve.

Slow Cooker Italian Beef Stew

Serves 6

2 tsp. Italian seasoning

¼ tsp. pepper

1 onion

12 oz. beef gravy

2stalks celery

1 lb. beef stew meat

19 oz. White kidney beans

1 tsp. beef base

2 c. green beans

2 c. carrots

2 garlic cloves

1 tsp. sugar

28 oz. crushed tomatoes in puree

All the ingredients go into the slow cooker for 10 to 12 hours giving the ingredients time to marinate and soften. Add sugar and frozen green beans. Cover and cook for 15 minutes.

Slow Cooker Mexican Beef Stew

Serves 6

2 lb. beef stew meat

28 oz. organic diced tomatoes

1 c. frozen small whole onions

1 tsp. chili powder

11 oz. whole kernel corn

15 oz. black beans

1 oz. taco seasoning mix

Mix all the ingredients except taco seasoning mix, black beans and corn in the cooker and cook for 11 hours. Stir up taco seasoning mix, black beans and corn. Cover and cook for 20 to 25 minutes on high heat setting.

Slow Cooker Cajun Beef Stew

Serves 4

¼ c. Caribbean jerk marinade

1 ½ lb. beef stew meat

1/3 c. all-purpose flour

4 Medium sized red potatoes

1 tbsp. Cajun seasoning

14.5 oz. tomatoes

3 c. frozen bell pepper and onion stir-fry

Coat your beef with the marinade. Add tomatoes, potatoes, flour and Cajun seasoning, and beef into the marinade. Heat for 7 to 8 hours on low. Add vegetables, heat up until vegetables are tender. Cool slightly and serve warm.

Slow Cooker Hungarian Beef Stew

Serves 6

1 c. frozen small whole onions

1 tbsp. paprika

½ c. sour cream

2 lb. beef stew meat

6 unpeeled new potatoes

¼ tsp. caraway seed

1 ½ c. frozen sweet peas

½ tsp. peppered seasoned salt

¼ c. all-purpose flour

1 ¾ c. beef flavored broth

Add the beef, potatoes, onions, flour, paprika, broth, peppered seasoned salt and caraway seed into the slow cooker, and stir until well mixed. Cook on low heat for 7 to 8 hours. Stir in the peas and sour cream. Cover and cook on low heat setting about 15 minutes more.

Chicken

Slow Cooker Chicken Taco Soup

Serves 8

10 ounce diced tomatoes with green chilies

1 chopped onion

1 ounce chili beans

1.25 ounce taco seasoning

3 boneless chicken breasts

12 ounce beer

8 ounce tomato sauce

15 ounce black beans

15 ounce whole kernel corn

Place all of your ingredients into the crock pot, cover and cook for 5 hours. Remove the chicken breasts from the soup and allow them to cool long enough to be handled. Shred the chicken, then, stir the shredded chicken back into the soup, and continue cooking for 2 hours, serve hot.

Slow-Cooker Chicken-Pasta Soup

Serves 6

1 onion

4 carrots

4 stalks celery

6 boneless, skinless chicken thighs

2 bay leaves

2 garlic cloves

1/4 c. flat-leaf parsley

1/2 c. pasta

Crackers for serving

Salt and black pepper as desired

Place the chicken, carrots, celery, onion, garlic, bay leaves, 6 c. water, 1 tsp. salt, and ¼ tsp. pepper into the slow cooker. Cook, covered on high for 7 to 8 hours. Remove chicken. Add the pasta to the slow cooker and cook until tender, 15 to 20 minutes on low. When the pasta is cooked, stir the chicken into the soup along with the parsley. Serve with the crackers.

Slow Cooker Chicken Pot Pie Stew

Serves 16

1 tbsp. black pepper

10 red potatoes

8 ounce baby carrots

4 boneless chicken breasts

1 tsp. celery salt

2 tsp. garlic salt

26 ounce cream of chicken soup

6 cubes chicken bouillon

1 c. chopped celery

16 ounce frozen mixed vegetables

Place the chicken, potatoes, carrots, celery, chicken soup, chicken bouillon, garlic salt, celery salt, and black pepper in a slow cooker on high for 5 hours. Mix the frozen mixed vegetables into the slow cooker, and cook 1 hour more.

Slow Cooker Chicken and Ramen Noodle Soup

Serves 6

1 fresh baby carrot

8-oz. sliced bamboo shoots

1 ¼ lb. boneless chicken thighs

8-oz water chestnuts

1/2 c. chopped stalk celery

3-oz ramen noodle soup oriental-flavor

1 c. frozen Sugar Snap Peas

32-oz chicken broth

2 green onions

Put all the ingredients, except the noodles and peas, into the slow cooker. Cover and cook for 7 to 8 hours. Then toss noodles into soup. Stir in the peas and cook for 10 minutes. If desired, add salt and pepper to taste.

Slow Cooker Chicken and Gnocchi Soup

Serves 6

9 oz. frozen baby sweet peas

1 c. julienne carrots

1 ¼ lb. boneless skinless chicken thighs

16 oz. gnocchi

1 tsp. dried thyme leaves

½ c. chopped onion

½ c. chopped celery

32 oz. chicken broth

10 3/4 oz. condensed cream of mushroom with roasted garlic soup

Cook your chicken for 5 to 7 minutes in a frying pan. Add chicken and remaining ingredients in the crock pot. Cover; cook on Low heat setting 8 to 10 hours. Stir in gnocchi and peas. Increase heat setting to High. Cover and cook until gnocchi and peas are tender. Add salt if desired.

Slow Cooker Italian Chicken Stew

Serves 6

19-oz Cannelloni Beans

15.5 /15-oz Kidney Beans

1 c. chopped celery

1 tbsp. sugar

2 small garlic cloves

4 boneless chicken breast halves

1 c. sliced carrots

3 tbsp. tomato paste

14.5-oz diced tomatoes

½ c. dry red wine

1 c. water

1 ½ tsp. dried Italian seasoning

Mix your chicken, cannellini beans, tomatoes, kidney beans, celery, garlic and carrots in the crock pot. Mix together all ingredients; mix well in a mixing bowl. Pour over the chicken and vegetables; mix well. Cook on low setting for 8 to 10 hours and serve hot.

Vegetables

Slow-Cooker White Bean and Kielbasa Stew

Serves 6

4 c. chicken stock

1 tsp. rosemary (dried)

1 lb. white beans (dried)

14 oz. sliced kielbasa

1 chopped yellow onion

14.5-oz. diced tomatoes

5 oz. baby spinach

6 garlic cloves

Combine your beans with the sliced kielbasa, chicken stock broth, diced tomatoes (and juices), onion, rosemary, garlic and 1 c. water in crock pot. Cover it and cook until the beans are tender, on low for 7 to 8 hours. Just before serving, stir in the spinach. Serve with bread.

Slow-Cooker Vegetable Stew

Serves 6

16-ounce chickpeas

4 carrots (2-inch pieces)

2 turnips (1-inch cubes)

1 onion

1/4 tsp. red pepper flakes

1/2 tsp. ground cumin

2 garlic cloves

1 1/2-inch slices of zucchini

1 c. mixed vegetable

14-ounce diced tomatoes

1 tsp. kosher salt

Begin by combining all the ingredients, except zucchini and chickpeas, in your crock pot. Cook on low heat for 6 hours, then, add in zucchini and chickpeas and cook for another hour on low. Serve hot.

Slow Cooker Creamy Potato Soup

Serves 6

2 c. water

10.5 ounce chicken broth

1 onion

6 slices bacon

5 large potatoes

12 fluid ounce evaporated milk

2 c. half-and-half cream

1/2 c. all-purpose flour

1/2 tsp. ground white pepper

1/2 tsp. dried dill weed

1/2 tsp. salt

Begin by cooking your bacon and onion in a frying pan until the bacon is evenly brown and the onions are soft. Transfer the bacon and onion to a slow cooker and stir in chicken broth, water, potatoes, salt, dill weed, and white pepper. Cook for 6 to 7 hours. Stir into the soup the flour, half-and-half and the evaporated milk. Cook for 30 minutes and serve hot.

Slow Cooker Vegetable Soup with Barley

Serves 10

1 c. sliced celery

1 onion

1 ½ c. baby-cut carrots

½ tsp. fennel seed

1 dried bay leaf

2 cloves garlic

6 c. water

1 c uncooked regular pearl barley

½ c. chopped green bell pepper

1 Peeled dark-orange sweet potato

1 ½ c. frozen corn

14.5 oz. diced tomatoes with basil, garlic and oregano

1 ½ c. frozen cut green beans

¼ tsp. Salt & pepper

Begin by layering all of the ingredients, except the tomatoes, in the crock pot but do not stir. Cover and cook on low for 6 to 8 hours. Stir the tomatoes into soup. Heat it for 10 minutes. Remove the bay leaf before serving.

Slow Cooker Vegetable Rice Soup

Serves 7

3 carrots, chopped

28 oz. organic diced tomatoes

28 oz. vegetable broth

3 zucchini

¼ c. chopped fresh basil leaves

1 c. uncooked instant rice

8 green onions

¼ tsp. pepper

1 tsp. salt

1 yellow bell pepper

2 tsp. dried marjoram leaves

2 cloves garlic

2 c. shredded cabbage

Put all the ingredients except rice and basil, into the crock pot. Cook for 6 to 8 hours on low. Stir in rice. Cook for about 15 minutes. Stir in the basil and serve hot.

Split Pea Soup

Serves 4-6

1 ½ c. chopped onion

4 carrots diced

16 oz. split peas

½ tsp. pepper

1 tsp. salt

6 c. hot water

3 garlic cloves minced

1 bay leaf

Start by layering the ingredients into the crock pot, starting with the peas. (Do not stir). Leave them to cook 8 to 10 hours on the low setting. Serve hot!

Tangy Black Bean Soup

Serves 6

1 lbs. black beans

1 red bell pepper seeded and diced

2 cloves garlic chopped

15 oz. diced drained tomatoes

1 tsp. cinnamon

4 c. vegetable broth

1 orange- juiced

1 tbsp. cumin

1 tsp. chipotle chili

1 tsp spice

Begin by soaking your black beans overnight or alternatively, boil water with the beans for at least 10 minutes, then leave them to soak for an hour more in a covered pot. Put the soaked and drained black beans into a 6-quart crock pot with the tomatoes, garlic, bell pepper, dried spices, orange and lime juice. Stir in the broth and thoroughly mix all the ingredients. Cover and cook for 8 to 10 hours on low. Serve and enjoy.

Confetti Yellow Pea Soup

Serves 6

4 c. water

¼ tsp. pepper

16 oz. dried yellow split peas, rinsed

10 1/2 oz. condensed chicken broth

1 c. carrots

6 oz. chorizo sausage

11 oz. whole kernel corn

½ c. sliced green onions

¼ tsp. salt

Red and green peppers to taste

Begin by combining all of your ingredients, except the onions and corn, in a crock pot. Cover; cook on low for 7 to 9 hours, or until peas are soft. Stir in onions and corn and allow to cook for another half hour. Serve.

Crock Pot Tomato-Basil Soup

Serves 4-6

4 cloves garlic, peeled but whole

2 sweet onions diced

3 carrots finely diced

3 tbsp. olive oil

1 tsp. red pepper flakes

1 tbsp. salt

1 Liter Vegetable broth

3 24 oz. whole peeled tomatoes

Basil leaf for serving

Place all of your ingredients into the slow cooker and set to low for 7 to 8 hours giving the ingredients time to marinate and soften in the tomato broth. Allow the soup to cool and then puree it until smooth and creamy in texture. Simmer until ready to serve.

French Onion Soup

Serves 4-6

1 ½ tsp. Dijon mustered

¼ c. red table wine

4 sliced onions

6 ½ c. vegetable broth

¾ tsp. thyme

2 bay leaves

1 ½ tsp. balsamic vinegar

Pepper to taste

Salt to taste

Place all the ingredients into a crock pot and leave to simmer for 4 or 5 hours oh high. Serve hot.

Slow Cooker Mediterranean Stew

Serves 10

10 ounce frozen okra

2 c. zucchini

1 butternut squash

1 sliced carrot,

1/2 c. vegetable broth

1 tomato

1/4 tsp. paprika

1/4 tsp. ground cinnamon

1/4 tsp. crushed red pepper

1 c. chopped onion

1/2 tsp. ground turmeric

1/2 tsp. ground cumin

2 c. eggplant, with peel

8 ounce tomato sauce

1/3 c. raisins

1 garlic clove

Place all of the ingredients into a crock pot and cook for 8-10 hours on low. Cook until vegetables are tender. Serve and enjoy.

Potato-Leek Soup

Serves 6

3 chopped carrots

4 peeled potatoes

2 leeks

2 chopped celery stacks

6 c. vegetable broth

2 cloves garlic minced

Salt and pepper to taste

Garnish For serving

Place all of your ingredients into the crock pot and add just enough liquid bullion to cover the vegetables, then cook for 4 to 6 hours on high. Use an emersion blender, a food processor, or a potato masher to puree the ingredients while in the crock pot. Add salt and pepper to taste, ladle into bowls and add an optional garnish of parsley.

Miscellaneous

Cheesy Brat Stew for the Slow Cooker

Serves 6

15 oz. green beans

6 browned bratwurst links,

4 peeled potatoes,

1 tbsp. dried minced onion

10.75 ounce cream of mushroom soup

2 c. shredded Cheddar cheese

1 red bell pepper

2/3 water

Place all of your ingredients into the slow cooler and cook for about 6 hours on low heat. Serve and enjoy.

Mushroom Lentil Barley Stew

Serves 8

3/4 c. dry lentils

3 bay leaves

2 tsp. ground black pepper

1 tsp. dried basil

2 tsp. dried summer savory

2 tsp. minced garlic

2 c. sliced fresh button mushrooms

1 ounce dried shiitake mushrooms, broken into pieces

2 quarts vegetable broth

3/4 c. uncooked pearl barley

1/4 c. dried onion flakes

Salt to taste

Mix all of the ingredients together in a crock pot and cook for 10- 12 hours on low. Don't forget to remove bay leaves before serving.

Slow Cooker Italian Chicken-Lentil Soup

Serves 6

4 sliced carrots

1 chopped onion

1 chopped zucchini

1 lb. boneless chicken thighs

8 oz. dried lentils

3 oz. sliced mushrooms

28 oz. diced tomatoes

¼ tsp. pepper

1 tbsp. dried basil leaves

½ tsp. salt

4 ½ c. chicken broth

Place all of the ingredients, except mushrooms and tomatoes, into the crock pot. Cook for 5 to 6 hours on high. Remove the chicken and shred it. Combine mushrooms, chicken and tomatoes in the crock pot again, set to low heat, and cook for another 14 minutes. Add basil and serve.

Slow Cooker Italian Ravioli Stew

Serves 6

19 oz. beans (cannellini)

2 c. sliced carrots,

1 c. chopped onion

29 oz. diced tomatoes with Italian-style herbs

2 tsp. dried basil leaves

28 oz. chicken broth

9 oz. cheese-filled ravioli

Combine all of your ingredients into a crock pot, except ravioli, and cook until vegetables are tender (about 7 hours). Increase heat setting to High, stir in the ravioli and cook about 8 minutes longer. Serve and enjoy.

Slow Cooker Italian Meatball Soup

Serves 6

14.5 oz. diced tomatoes with basil, garlic and oregano

1 c. water

1 ¾ c. beef flavored broth

16 oz. frozen cooked Italian meatballs

19 oz. beans, drained (cannellini

1/3 c. shredded Parmesan cheese

Place all of your ingredients, except cheese, in the slow cooker. Leave it to cook for 8 to 10 hours on low. Add cheese before serving.

Slow Cooker Vegetable Beef Soup

Serves 6

1 tsp. seasoned salt

4 cloves garlic

1/2 c. onion, chopped

1 1/2 c. red potatoes

1 lb. beef stew meat

2 c. frozen mixed vegetables

2 bay leaves

28 oz. beef broth

14 oz. diced tomatoes

15 to 16 oz. northern beans

½ tsp. pepper

Begin by placing all of your ingredients into the slow cooker, except the frozen veggies. Set to low and cook for 7 to 8 hours. Add in the mixed vegetables and increase the heat to high. Cover and cook until vegetables are tender. Don't forget to remove bay leaves before serving.

Slow Cooker Beefy French Onion Soup

Serves 6

1 ½ lb. beef stew meat

2 dried bay leaves

2 tbsp. sugar

1 tbsp. butter

7 c. onions

32 oz. condensed beef consommé

1 c. apple juice

8 oz. shredded Swiss cheese

¼ c. dry sherry

¼ tsp. dried thyme leaves

8 slices French bread

Place onions, butter and sugar, bay leaves and beef into the bottom of your crock pot. Cook for 9 to 10 hours on low until onions are deep brown, then, mix in the beef consommé, sherry, apple juice and thyme and increase heat setting to high. Cover and cook 10 minutes. Remove bay leaves to serve.

Slow Cooker Lentil and Ham Soup

Serves 6

1 1/2 c. diced cooked ham

1 c. chopped celery

1 c. chopped onion

1/4 tsp. dried thyme

1 c. chopped carrots

1 c. dried lentils

1/4 tsp. black pepper

2 garlic cloves

8 tsp. tomato sauce

1 c. water

1 bay leaf

32 oz. chicken broth

1/2 tsp. dried oregano

1/2 tsp. dried basil

Combine all the ingredients and cook on low for 11 hours. Discard the bay leaf before serving. Enjoy.

Slow-Cooker Tortilla Soup with Pork and Squash

Serves 6

3-lb. boneless pork butt

1 tbsp. canola oil

14.5-ounce tomatoes

1 1/2 lb. 1-inch pieces butternut squash

2 garlic cloves

1 tbsp. chili powder

1 jalapeño pepper

4 6-inch corn tortillas strips

4 c. Water

Kosher salt for taste

Lime wedges and sliced radishes

Toss all of your ingredients in the crock pot and cook for 7-8 hours on low. Check if the pork is tender, then, put the tortillas in and bake with canola oil and add salt until crispy. Cook for 8 to 10 minutes in high heat setting. Serve and enjoy.

Slow-Cooker Black Bean and Beer-Braised Pork Soup

Serves 6

24-oz. your choice of beer

1 lb. dried black beans

1 tsp. ground cumin

1 1/2 lb. boneless pork butt

1 chopped onion

1/2 c. refrigerated salsa

1 tbsp. adobo sauce

1 tbsp. chopped canned chipotle

1/4 c. cilantro

1/2 c. sour cream

Kosher salt as desired

Place the beer, 3 c. water, the chilies, the adobo sauce, the ground cumin, pork, beans, onions, and 1 1/2 tsp. salt. Cook for 5 hours. Serve with the sour cream, salsa, and cilantro.

Slow-Cooker White Bean Soup

Serves 6

1 tbsp. red wine vinegar

1 onion

1/2 lb. Andouille sausage links

4 sprigs thyme

8 c. chicken broth

1 lb. dried white beans

8 c. collard greens only leaves

Small quantity olive oil

Small quantity bread sticks

2 stalks celery

Kosher salt and black pepper to taste

Place all the ingredients, except vinegar, into the crock pot and cook until the greens are tender. Remove the thyme stems, add the vinegar, salt and pepper or according to your requirement and serve with bread sticks.

Conclusion:

Thank you for taking this journey through delicious crock pot cooking with us. We hope you have found some new favorite recipes that you can share with friends and enjoy for years to come. With these slow-cooker soups and stew recipes, you can prepare healthy and affordable meals without spending lots of time in the kitchen. There is nothing quite as welcoming as walking into a home filled with the aromas of delicious food and these recipes will surely serve that purpose. Happy cooking to you!

8350113R00025

Printed in Great Britain
by Amazon.co.uk, Ltd.,
Marston Gate.